LOVE *and* LIFE

JEREMIAH WILLIAMS

PublishAmerica
Baltimore

Softcover 9781462689002
PUBLISHED BY PUBLISHAMERICA, LLLP
www.publishamerica.com
Baltimore

Printed in the United States of America

LOVE

Be My Wife

Humbly I fall before my love and ask her hand
Knees so weak I can hardly stand
My hearts pounding, I've blocked out all my surroundings
My focus is on you and you alone
Every moment a treasure, every kiss I cherish
Give me your hand and I'll give you my heart
Come with me and we'll never be apart
Take this ring, my heart and my life
I'm ready to start living, but not without you
Be my wife

Beauty of the Sunset

I watch the beauty of the sun setting on the ocean
As the waves crash and the wind softly blows the clouds in motion
The sun slowly vanishes into the horizon
Giving way to a brilliant sky full of purple and red colors schemes
Fading into a blue so beautiful it could make the darkest soul glow
Slowly the night takes hold and the stars begin to appear
The moon dimly shines onto the water and all my worries disappear
I close my eyes as a calm wind hits my face stopping me in my tracks
I open them to a gentle peace
It's the simple things in life that set you free
The world is a beautiful place and love has a beautiful face

Daddy's Boy

Little fingers, little toes
Every time daddy sees you, his face glows
Chubby little cheeks
Sweet little nose
No other son would daddy have chose

Soft and sweet
Cute and cuddly
Daddy loves you so much
My little bubby

A gift from God
A pleasure to receive
A blessing from heaven
You given to me

Daddy's little boy
Daddy's love
Daddy's sweet gift, sent from above

Dream Girl

A beautiful girl, confident and smart
Exceedingly beautiful, she's stolen my heart
A strut in her step, a sway in her hips
Temptations gleam at the lick of her lips
Scent like rain, touch like fire
Making her mine is my only desire
Butterflies in my stomach, my palms begin to sweat
I need her in my life, she's as good as it gets
Hear my plea, I fall to my knee
Take this ring, and marry me

Love At Last

I wish there was a way to express to you how I feel
To show you this love for you is real
I can't express in words my thoughts
Or how long for this love I've fought

The thoughts are many
The words are few
The words I need to show my love for you
I give my heart, to you my love
The one God sent from up above

My angel, my heart
I was yours all along
Right from the start
With you is where I belonged

Your love cuts deeper than any love I've ever known
It heals the cuts from my past
You're the only girl I've ever truly loved
And it's a love that I want to last

Fall

The sun brightly shines through the trees
The wind moves effortlessly through the leaves
The branches dance and sing
Fall is back again in the forest
Red and orange purple and yellow
Cool breezes blow as temperatures mellow

Old fades and withers so new life can form
Nature takes its course
Deer frolic in the meadows
Moose graze in the shallows
Majestic mountains all a glow
With the fresh white powder of October snow

The sun slowly disappears into the night
A harvest moon glows orange and bright
Coyote's howl and raccoon's prowl
Owls hoot in the trees
Leaves clamor in the breeze
Seasons change, each one magical in its own way

Far Away

You never realize how much you love someone until you
don't see them as much
The times you realize they're too far to touch
Far away where I can't see your faces
I'm learning on my own now how to run life's races
I couldn't have asked for better parents or a better family
than the one I have and treasure
I'm thankful to be a part of this family forever
Thank you for being the best parents you could possibly be
I'm proud to be a part of this family tree

Heaven Foretold

Heaven on earth, you're like heaven to hold
We belong together, heaven foretold
From the moment I saw you,
I knew it was true
From heaven you were sent
From heaven to hold
Forever you're mine
Forever to hold
Forever mine, for heaven foretold
So perfectly meshed
So perfectly timed
The day heaven foretold
That you would be mine

I Promise

I promise to love you, to cherish you
I promise to never leave your side, come what may
I will always thank God for my precious gift he promised to
provide
My love for you will never fade, will never die, never will
you cry

This I promise you
I will love you and I will cherish you all the days of my life
You are a precious gem, a beautiful flower whose beauty
never fades
You're my best friend, my wife, and the love of my life

My heart melts when I'm near you
And thanks God for you every second I'm not
My love will never fail you
This my vow
To let the light of my love shine upon you when all else fades

I've Loved You Before

4 years together, but somehow I feel I've loved you longer
In my dreams, in my thoughts, before I ever heard you speak
In another life, another form, I've loved you before
Before there was time, before the stars were aligned
Before the dark, before the light, somehow before
In spirit form we were together, somehow meshed together
Our souls were one before we ever met, ever touched
Forever you've been the one I've loved so much
The missing half of me, my best friend
The one I've loved from the beginning and will until the very
end

Lost In Love

I've walked to close to the brook of love
And now I've fallen in
Swept off my feet
You stole my heart and everything within

Lost in love, I don't wanna be found
My heart longs to be yours
I'll follow the sound

Of our hearts beating faster
Our breaths getting deeper
I want you in my arms

Be mine tonight
Make me your man
It's the only thing that's right
Give me your hand

Marry me my love
Come into my life
Take me as your husband
I take you as my wife

Love

So much love within my soul
I don't know how, but you make my heart beat fast and slow
A love so warm I never wanna leave
You as mine is hard to believe

Burn, burn, burn goes my heart around you
A love forever, forever so true
Pound, pound, pound goes my heart around you
Never to leave as sure as the sky is blue

You are mine and I am yours
Your love is as warm as Florida shores
Love is patient, love is kind
Slow to anger and quick to forgive

You are my heart, my soul, my best friend, and my wife
I am so thankful you're a part of my life

Love at first Sight

Love at first sight
A feeling unknowingly taking over me
Unexpected, unrealistic, unexplainably consuming me
Impossible to be true, there's no chance

All control is lost
This feeling has me hostage
I love you is all I can say
It's the only word that makes any sense

This feeling is pure bliss
I hang on every kiss
Your face I long to touch
Your hand I long to hold

I try to speak, but the words elude me
My palms are moist with anticipation
My heart beats like a doves wings
My spirit sings to the world, you're mine

Marriage

Wife-
The years have gone by us so fast
The memories are many, but our love has past
I can't remember the last time you kissed me goodnight
The last time you said I love you just to say it

What happened to "us"?
Between the kids and work, our love has gone cold
I don't know what to think
I'm beginning to fold

I guess I just need to accept the one thing I've dreaded...
That our love has faded and will never be the same again...
So I'll pack my bags so we can move on with our lives

Where has the time gone?
Our love was so strong
Where did I go wrong?

She's lost that look in her eye
The one that says, I'll love you till I die
I know things have been tough
That this road we've chosen has been rough
Between the bills and our kids we've lost that spark
I guess our love has gone dark...

Husband-
I've lost sight of who we were
Tell me that it's not too late
That I didn't lose you too

Wife-
My bags are packed, our love has gone
The fire has left, our love has moved on
You said you would love me forever
That your love would never leave
You say you still love me, please make me believe

Husband-
My wife,
Forever I will love you, forever I will stay
I will be here for you each coming day
I love you with all my heart and soul
Your love completes me, consumes me whole
My love has never ceased, has never stopped growing
I meant forever when I asked you to be my wife
That I wanted to be with you for the rest of my life

Husband-
Down to my knees I fall
Please marry me again
Before we lose it all

Wife-
I will marry you
Tonight, we renew our vows
Our love is new again
And with our love we move on

Meant to Be

This love is deep,
This love is true
Everywhere I've looked
But no one compares to you
We were meant to be
Meant to touch
Meant to share
So much in love

Take my heart
Take my hand
No one else comes close
No one else can
You're my heart, my soul
You make my heart beat out of control

You were my first
You are my love
Warm like the sun, shines like the moon
Beautiful love song
Our hearts perfectly in tune

O Child of Mine

O child of mine
How you warm my heart
How can I love you so much?
That I'd rather put my desires aside
And let you guide

O child of mine
It won't be long before you grow into a warrior
Please take your time

O child of mine
Soon you'll no longer be mine
But a warrior for God
To fight and win souls for the kingdom of God

Remember deep inside though
You'll always be a child of mine

Proposal

Love, in a moment of suspended hope flies free
Spreads its wings and soars above the trees
Melts your heart and takes your breath away

Pull in close for a kiss and lose all feeling
The goose bumps fill your body
A cool chill runs down your spine

The sparks start flying as your hands touch
And you know she's the one
Your heart starts to flutter out of control
As a deep joy bubbles up from your soul

Down on your knees you fall
As you risk it all in a moments touch
Will you marry me?
Her eyes grow big as she covers her mouth
Long silence...yes, and the story begins

Pure Bliss

The stillness of night
Me holding you tight
My hand in yours
And yours in mine

A perfect moment of pure bliss
You steal my heart with every kiss
With every touch a chill runs down my spine
An electric pulse through my entire body

A love like the stars
Infinite and beautiful
Your love replaces my scars
With a feeling so magical

Your eyes sparkle like diamonds
Your laugh is intoxicating
Smile and my worries disappear
Because I know this love is forever

A feeling I never want to end
Flowing like the wind
Romantic and free
The way God intended it
No rules, just love

Quinlan

I remember the day so clear
When I was given a gift so dear
Little onesies kept in a box
A little red ribbon graced the top

Greatest gift I could ever receive
A beautiful baby boy has been given to me
A precious gift, wrapped in love
Sealed with a kiss, sent from above
Soft to touch, warm to hold
All it took was one look
And I was sold

So long have I imagined your face
Wondered how you would cry
Wondered about the color of your eyes
Who you would be when you got older

Time passes slowly, longing to hold you,
Kiss you, snuggle you, feel your warmth
We all anxiously await your arrival
Trying to pass the time until you're in our arms

The Moment I Laid Eyes On you

I walked in and there you were
Walking out on stage, an angel I'm sure
Stopped in my tracks, you brought my world to a halt
The moment I laid eyes on you, I knew the result
You were my wife, the one I've longed for my whole life
The one I can't live my life without

How did this happen?
Love this complex doesn't happen over night
But for me it happened in an instance
The moment I saw you
The moment I laid eyes on you, I knew
You would be that one love I would die to lose

I had to know your name, had to hear your voice
I simply had to stay and see what happened
I simply had no choice
I knew you were the one before I ever heard you speak
Knew you would be my wife before your love I ever seeked

Finally I gave you my number and 6 hours later we hung up
the phone
From that moment on, I knew, I would never again be alone
I told you my heart, that you tore my world apart
I wanted you as my wife, and I wouldn't settle for less

I asked your hand and you gave it to me
I asked for your heart and you said it's yours
I asked for your life and you said on one condition
You give me yours

Unforgettable Days

Nine months of excitement
Hours of torment
Days of enjoyment
Here you are

Brown eyes, brown hair
Looking like mommy and daddy
My baby boy
You bring so much joy

From the first you smiled
Your cheeks puffed
Your eyes disappear
In my heart life appears

It's amazing how much you bring to my everyday
In which I say
You'll bring more unforgettable days

Valentine

I've struggled for so long
To sing this life song
I tried to find the words
And failed to play the chords
But one day I just gave it all up
I said Lord, here's my life, take it from me

He tuned my life to the sound of his will
And he put in my life this beautiful girl
Seeing her that first night she took my breath away
I tried to speak, but had nothing to say
You're the girl I've always wanted
But couldn't find on my own
You're the one person who can make my life complete
The only one who can make my heart skip a beat

I've searched for you all my life
And now that I've found you, I never wanna let you go
You're the girl I want for all time
So this I ask, will you be my valentine?

Wild Love

You're the one I've been dreaming of
Been searching for my entire life
Sent from the heavens above, an angel I'm sure
My relief from loneliness, your love is the cure

Your love is like air
I need you to breathe
You've captured my heart
Now I believe

Come and run away with me
We'll go where the wild flowers thrive
Where no one can find us
Where we can feel alive

We'll live in the mountains
Climb in the trees
Drink from waterfalls
Come be with me

No rhyme or reason
Just you and me
Completely free

LIFE

A Cure for Cancer

Every one of us has gone astray
But one was sent to wipe our tears away
We were a people who were lost and without hope
We had nowhere to go and no way to cope
We cried out with no answer
Life without Christ is like cancer
Eating away at your heart and soul
He's the only one that can make you whole
One day God answered our call
He sent the one that would save us all
He died and was risen on the third day
Completely wiping our sins away

Amazing Love

What have I done to deserve such a love?
Reigning down each day from heaven above
What have I done to deserve such a thing?
For all of my life I have caused you such pain
The reason you chose me I don't understand
But this much I know, saving my soul took just one man

Beautiful Savior

The beauty of a rose captured in His face
Knowing that our sins could be erased
His face shone with light as He hung from a tree
Knowing that He was dying for me
His arms stretched out and nailed to the cross
Dying for us was the ultimate cost

Fight for Your Life

You've turned your back on God
He'll never forgive you
Come with me and be free
I will give you untold riches
Anything that you want
Come and follow me

Death at every side
Nowhere to run or hide
Death at every glance
You never even had a chance
I know your weaknesses

Turn your back on me?
I own you, you belong to me
Just the two of us in this room
I will be the death of you
But you can't escape me

We're meshed together, forever
I control you know, you're mine
I will hold on to you until the end of time
I am your identity now, put on your mask
You can act like you're someone else
But I know your true identity

Take the blade and cut out your heart
Jump in the fire, let it consume every part
Hand over your soul, you're under my control
You gave me this power
I won't let go without a fight
And trust me; it will be a fight for your life

God's Love

Your love never fails, never gives an inch on those it seeks,
never pales, surrenders or gives up.
Your love is strong, knocks down my defenses, my walls,
never weakens, and never dulls.
Your love is pure, white as snow, clear as glass, brighter than
a polished diamond ring, makes my soul sing,
To you my spirit clings, gasps for air, cries for more, longs to
touch, grasps for strength.
Your love holds my every need, my deepest desire, Lord you
are my fire, the reason I breathe,
The inspiration pushing me to keep going. Keep praying.
Keep growing.

Lord your love is everything, consumes me, bonds me, frees
me, puts me to death, brings me to life.
You are the air I breathe, the water I drink, the very life
inside of me.
Father, you are what this world needs, the hope of a
generation, last breath for mankind.
Died and rose, had everything, but death you chose, three
days and you stole the keys to death and my heart,
Never to be apart, forever together.

O how my soul sings, your love is a song,
A song the world desperately needs to hear.
Let me sing your love song to all who will listen.
Give them ears to hear, eyes to see, fingers to touch,
And a heart to feel, show them you're real.
Peel back the layers of their heart and ignite a spark.
Let it consume them until there's nothing left.

Let the world see you in their every word, their every action, cause a love reaction,
An electric pulse surging through their body, a jolt of life, cut through them like a knife.
Father let your spirit rise in me, cause a fire that will ignite this nation and consume the world.
Raise me up to be a mighty soldier, a force to be reckoned with,
a wrecking ball for all the devils plans for people's lives.

May the devil be confused, lost, chaos take over his kingdom, souls lost at every turn?
Another log to burn for the cause of the savior. You his only concern. His beloved creation.
Created and lost, brought back to life by grace, died and revived by mercy, love abounding never failing,
But always prevailing, an unstoppable force, all powerful, all knowing, forgetful of sin,
And mindful of you his beloved creation.

He Is Real

Wide expanses full of bright stars
Planets beyond comprehension
Suns burn millions of miles away
Yet we deny your existence

Oceans roar and eagles soar defying gravity
Leaves change and flowers bloom
Yet we believe in the big boom
Rains fall and rainbows glow in all their magnificent color
The earth screams of your existence, but no one listens
Too busy with life to care how we got here

Earths quake and mountains shake
The Lord is on his way
Open your ears and listen to what is being said
They say you're a fairy tale, they say you're dead
So how come I can't get this feeling out of my head
Jesus is coming, Jesus is real
How will you handle it, how will you deal
When the God you say is dead comes back in the middle of
your busy life
A thief in the night

Wake up to the truth before you perish in a lie
Question what you hear before it catches you off guard
Know where you stand or trust what you think you already know
Just be sure you know where you'll go

Heart of Love

Love is an amazing feeling that holds a much greater high
than hate or greed ever could
Love knows no enemies and sees potential in all to do good
Love is a sweet sweet taste in your mouth
Love is forever, undying, unrelenting, never ending
Love doesn't give up when things get hard
It holds out til there's nothing left to give
Love gives of itself and expects nothing in return
Love is patient, love is kind
Love hopes all things, endures all things until nothing else
remains

Hero

This world is hurting
This world is a mess
Can anyone save us
From our brokenness?

Why should we run
A hero has come
The one true savior
Protector of mankind

He's come to save the day
To take our pain away
Give him your mess
And he will make a masterpiece
Give him your life
And he will set you free

Ask him to show you the way
And he will guide your feet
Ask him how much he loves you
And he replies,
Three nails pierced my hands and feet

I Want To Give Up

Today another screw up
Tomorrow another heartbreak
Why do I do the things I hate?
Why do I always get so far just to fall short?
Will I ever get to a place where I can't fall?
Will I ever be able to stand tall?
Today I feel like giving up
And tomorrow will never be enough

I Want To Know You More

Who are you God?
Where can I find you?
I want so much more than to read about you in stories I don't
understand
I want to know you better than my best friend

I want to know you God
I want to know you care
I want to be like you, but I don't know how
I'm not perfect, though I give it my all
I always fall

I know you're real, but I don't know how to find you
I know you love me, but I don't know how to love you
I've climbed the mountain in search of you before
But I always get scared and climb back down

I want to know you, show me how to find you
I want to love you, teach me how to love

I Will Carry You Home

Time doesn't feel real
My life is a blur
I'm trying to seal the deal
I finally found the cure

I've found the answers to all my questions
But something's pulling me down
I thought I finally learned my lesson
But something still has me bound

I'm upset and I don't know why
I can't seem to change
I look around as I start to cry
Because hope seems out of range

I walk alone as I try to figure this out
I see something coming my way
My heart is full of doubt, as a hand reaches out
From a cloud of light, showing me the way

A voice like thunder comes from the figure of a man
Out of fear and comfort I take his hand
He throws me over his shoulder and carries me through the
sand

He tells me everything will be alright
Don't worry about the things to come
If you ever get lost just come to the light
For there, I will be waiting to carry you home

Jesus Loves Me This I Know

Jesus loves me, this I know
Because the bible tells me so
He's opened my eyes so I can see
Only through him will I be free

Jesus loves me this I know
Where he leads me I will go
Born again, he's leading me home
This barren dessert no longer I rome

I once was lost but now I'm found
My broken life he turned around
I'm back on track, I'm ready to run
I'll chase after you, the holy one

Amazing grace how sweet the sound
My chains he broke that held me bound
Free from addiction, free from pain
Because the spotless lamb was slain

The Greatest Love Story Ever Told

2,000 years ago a savior came, took the blame,
The shame, and showed the devil why he's the name above
all names.
From heaven to earth to take the curse,
Destined from the day he was born,
Two nails and a crown of thorns.
Hung on a cross, all our sins were lost,
Put to death, brought to life,
Three days and his grave was empty.
Rose from the dead, and when all was said
He took back the keys of death, Satans breath.
Jesus came, gave, and the world was saved.
The greatest love story ever told.

My Life I Lay At Your Feet

I watch as the sun sets, giving way to night
I look at the sky, as the stars shine so bright
I watch as the wave's crash onto the shore
As the storm clouds roll in and the rain begins to pour
I look at you and you look at me
We both just smile because there's no place we'd rather be
I can't imagine my life without you
I don't know where I'd be or what I would do
Without you in my life, I just wouldn't be complete
Jesus you gave your life for me, my life I lay at your feet

My Spirit Awaken

I'm standing here looking at the stars in the sky
I scream out loud as I start to cry
My spirit cries out for more of you
But my flesh stops me short of pushing through
Each day the devil tells me more lies
Piercing my heart like a thousand knives
Nothing Satan can say will keep me from my goal
Never will he kill my soul
Jesus died to set me free
Satan had the power of death
But Jesus stole the key
Jesus won me through His death
And now I'll praise Him with every breath

Never Give Up

Never give up
No matter how hard your flesh tries to push
When it feels like there's no way out and you just wanna stop
Keep going
This world will tell you that's impossible
But do you think Jesus cared; he died and was risen on the third day
No one could make him stop believing
And no one can stop me
Only I can stop myself
There's no hope in this world
Because all hope lies in Jesus
For God so loved the world that he gave his one and only son that whoever believes in him shall not perish but have everlasting life.

Power In Christ

God this generation is in need of your awesome love
I pray for your mercy to fall on us
Give us words to speak and hearts for the lost
Let us have a love that never stops, no matter what the cost
God I desire a heart like yours
Full of love and compassion for all
I pray that you would open my eyes to your awesome power
Make your word come alive to me, I pray
I don't want to play hide and seek with you anymore
I seek after you for a time and then I run and hide
I want that to leave me, please God, set me free
My generation is dying around me everyday
But I do nothing to stop it because I don't believe
Remove the caulis from my eyes, o God
Allow me to see what you see
I know the very same power that lies in Jesus lies in me
Because he lives in me
I am not dead as I feel but I am alive
Where ever Jesus is there is life and power
And he lives in me

Pray

Take a look around, tell me what you see
When I look around I see the things I need
I see the things I want, but can't have

I woke up this morning with a different point of view
I looked around and saw a world that needs you
I saw people dying and going to hell
And I wasn't doing anything to stop it
I questioned myself, what can I do

Jesus simply said, pray
Pray for the lost and the sick
Pray for the ones that know the truth, but ignore it
Pray for the deceived and the hopeless

But don't just pray for the lost
Pray for the true followers of Christ
For if they hadn't answered Gods call no one would be saved

Prayer For A Lost Soul

Lord, I come before you longing to be yours
I'm through playing games
I've tried for so long to put you in my life
But there was a problem
My whole heart wasn't in it

I want to get rid of the filth, the dirt
All of this pain and hurt
Everything that keeps me from you
I'm done with running and making excuses
I want you in my life

You promised if I sought after you with my whole heart
I would find you
I want your presence
I wanna know your love and your face
Your loving mercy and your saving grace

I welcome you in my life
Cut away the sin from me
Come into my life and set me free

Take Me Higher

Love, true as time, free as air
Spread your awesome wings and fly free
High above the waters take me
To the highest mountain top
The deepest ocean take me

Take me high in the clouds
I'm lighter than air
Take me on your wings
To the place I wanna be

Floating on clouds
Flowing with the wind
Take me higher
Where there is no end

I wanna go higher into the heavens
Into the unknown
The places few have roamed
Take me there on your wings
Take me where I am free
Into the unseen

The End Is Near

Without Jesus the world is a mess
Don't hold your sins inside, confess
Give him your heart, time is running out
Jesus is coming soon, I have no doubt

The end is getting near
The time is uncertain, but the plan is clear
Take God out of our schools
Out of the White House
Out of control

Conspiracies cover ups, something's not right
They're trying to hide the truth
Feeding us lies
Abortions on the rise
Sexual compromise
How much more will God allow

Ready or not, here I come
Sound the trumpet and bang the drums
I come for my followers, not another one
You made your decision and now I'm done

One world order, you'll do what we say
Under our control, we won't let you pray
Take our mark or we'll take your life
Give us your allegiance or we'll take your wife

The end is near, it's already begun
Without Jesus, there will be nowhere to run

The Lamb That Was Slain

Your beauty transcends that of the entire earth
Your love goes beyond what I can see
The glory of the savior is brighter then the sun
And his mercy runs deeper then the sea
Willingly you came, and willingly you died
You died the cruelest death
But you never regretted a thing
I can't imagine how awful, how you endured all the pain
That glorious night when the lamb was slain
You came to offer your life for the entire world
So to you Lord my life I yield

The Perfect Love Story

I know a man named Jesus
When I was young I was taught about how he freed us
I was taught of his love
So pure and perfect
I was told of his mercy and grace
How the light shines so brightly from his face

Growing older I wondered
Why would a man who had no fault wanna die for me?
Because he was the only one who could set me free
The only man who could live his life out perfectly

Jesus knew he had to save the day
To come and die for you and me
The one true savior, the only way
To conquer death and set us free

The Savior Is Calling

God is calling you by name
This life you live is not a game
Hate and compromise will destroy your life
They'll cut you down just like a knife
This day you live could be your last
Your life could end in just a flash
Don't wait another day to give your heart
Every seconds uncertain when you're apart
God forgave you at the cross
With His last breath your sins were lost

We Have To Fight Back

To those true, die hard Jesus freaks
We must hold true to the end
We have to stay confident in the way we did when we first
gave our lives to the one true Savior
This world is dying around us
God's children are giving up because they don't know
We haven't done our job as believers to show them the love
of Christ
They are falling into the devils trap
He tells them that we don't love them, that we think we're
better than them
The church isn't standing up to him and fighting back
We're taking things too lightly
If we're going to save our lost brothers and sisters
We're going to have to fight
Not with mortal weapons in the natural
But with our sword and shield in the spiritual
We must show these people that we love them
That Jesus died for them, because he loves them
God must be shining from our being everyday
I am not speaking unrealistically, but literally glowing
People should see us walking down the street with light
shining off of us
They NEED to be drawn to the Savior who lives within us
If we don't stand up, who will?
You can't keep putting things off till tomorrow
When not even today is promised to you
There is a world full of hate and sorrow
So what will you do?
Choose this day whom you will serve
Fear or love

Would You

If I cried for help, would you save me?
If you thought there was something better for me
Would you set me free?
If I was lost and hurt
Would you show me the way?
If you had to die so I could live
Would you

Crying out, you heard me
Stuck in a mess of my own doing
You set me free
Lost and confused you shined your light
Being the only one who could save me
You gave your life

You Were There

You were there when my plans fell apart
You were there to mend my broken heart
Came to my rescue when I was lost
Gave your life for mine, to pay the cost

When I was lost and had nowhere to go
There you were
When I needed a shoulder to cry on
There you were
When I thought I had screwed up so bad that no one would
take me back
You took me back
And when I thought I couldn't hold the weight of this world
anymore
You said; let me carry it for you

CPSIA information can be obtained at www.ICGtesting.com
Printed in the USA
BVOW071903180912

300783BV00001B/160/P

9 781462 689002